2018
FIFA WORLD CUP
RUSSIA™

FIFA WORLD CUP
RUSSIA 2018

KIDS' HANDBOOK

Published under licence by Carlton Books Limited
© 2018 Carlton Books Limited,
20 Mortimer Street, London W1T 3JW

ISBN 978-1-78312-338-4
1 3 5 7 9 10 8 6 4 2
Printed in Dongguan, China

Writer: Kevin Pettman
Design: RockJaw Creative
Consultant: Cris Freddi

The publishers would like to thank the following sources for their kind
permission to reproduce the pictures in this book.

ALL © GETTY IMAGES
Page 4. Levi Bianco/LatinContent, 5. Shaun Botterill/FIFA, 6. Tasso Marcelo/AFP, 7. Javier Soriano/AFP,
8BL. Central Press, 8BR. Alexey Nasyrov/Anadolu Agency, 9. Stanislav Krasilnikov/TASS, 10L. Christof
Stache/AFP, 10R. Toshifumi Kitamura/AFP, 11TL. Quinn Rooney, 11BL. Martin Rose, 11BC. Christof Stache/
AFP, 11BR. Alexander Hassenstein/FIFA, 12. Adam Pretty, 13TR. Jamie McDonald, 13L. Stanislav Krasilnikov/
TASS, 14L. David Cannon, 14BR. Popperfoto, 15. Michael Urban/AFP, 16L. VI Images, 16R. Alex Livesey/FIFA,
16BR. Buda Mendes, 19. Chris Brunskill Ltd, 20C. Pedro Vilela, 20R. Mehdi Taamallah/NurPhoto, 20BL.
Ahmad Mora/NurPhoto, 21. AFP, 22. Shaun Botterill, 23. Jamie McDonald, 24R. Mike Hewitt, 24BL. Dursan
Aydemir/Anadolu Agency, 26. Mike Hewitt, 27. Carlos Rodrigues, 28-29. Jimmy Bolcina/Photonews, 28B.
Leonardo Fernandez/LatinContent, 29. Laurence Griffiths, 30. Claudio Villa, 31. Franck Fife/AFP, 32. Stuart
Franklin/Bongarts, 33. Jean Catuffe, 34TR. Jimin Lai/AFP, 34BL. Nagel/Sportbild/ullstein bild, 35. Sven
Nackstrand/AFP, 36R. Michael Regan, 36BL. Eric Renard/Corbis, 37. Mike Hewitt, 38. Peter Kovalev/TASS,
39. Ronald Martinez, 40. Ian Walton, 41T. Tim de Waele/Corbis, 41B. Robert Cianflone

Contents

Note to reader: the facts and records in this book are accurate as of 10 October 2017.

© FIFA TM

Welcome to Russia!

The 2018 FIFA World Cup™ promises to be the biggest and best football tournament ever – and your *Kids' Handbook* is the ultimate guide to the action! It is packed with players, teams, pictures, stats, facts, tips, trivia, puzzles, activities and results charts to fill in. Read on to discover everything you need to know about the 2018 FIFA World Cup!

Who is FIFA?

The Fédération Internationale de Football Association (FIFA) was founded in 1904 and is based in Zurich, Switzerland. It has 211 member associations. Amongst other football tournaments, FIFA organizes the FIFA World Cup every four years. In 2018 the competition is being held in Russia for the first time. FIFA picked Russia as the host nation way back in 2010. Since then the country has been busy building new stadiums, and upgrading existing ones, to get ready for the tournament.

When is it?

The action kicks off on 14 June at the 81,000-capacity Luzhniki Stadium in Moscow, the capital city of Russia. The following four weeks will be a total football festival as 64 matches are played around the country!

Where is it?

The 2018 FIFA World Cup matches are being played in 11 different cities in Russia. These are Moscow, Saint Petersburg, Kaliningrad, Saransk, Kazan, Sochi, Volgograd, Samara, Ekaterinburg, Rostov-on-Don and Nizhny Novgorod.

Will Neymar, the world's most expensive player, inspire Brazil to a record sixth FIFA World Cup?

Champions Germany are hoping to be the first team to defend the title since 1962.

Which countries are playing?

As early as March 2015, 208 national teams began playing qualifying games to reach the 2018 FIFA World Cup, with 32 finally gaining a place. The first team to qualify was Russia. That's because the host nation of a FIFA World Cup qualifies automatically! Brazil have won the FIFA World Cup a record five times and in March 2017 they were the first team to qualify from the South American group.

Fun at the FIFA World Cup™

With 64 matches being played, there will be at least 5,760 minutes of amazing football action at the 2018 FIFA World Cup! Each team will pick a squad of 23, which means 736 players will be in Russia plus hundreds more coaches and team staff.

© FIFA TM

Zabivaka says: More than one million Russians voted on FIFA.com to choose me as the 2018 FIFA World Cup mascot!

FIFA Fan Fests

For those fans in Russia who are not lucky enough to have a ticket to watch a game, there is another fun way to celebrate the FIFA World Cup. FIFA Fan Fests will be staged in all 11 host cities during the tournament. These are places where fans can watch matches on a large screen and also enjoy music, performances, food and drink, and other fun activities. Over five million people visited a FIFA Fan Fest at the 2014 FIFA World Cup.

Meet the mascot

A football-mad grey wolf called Zabivaka is the official mascot of the 2018 FIFA World Cup. He is a cheeky character who loves to kick a ball with his older brothers, sisters and friends. Zabivaka means 'the one who scores' in Russian – watch out for him popping up throughout your *Kids' Handbook* with lots of FIFA World Cup facts!

Zabivaka

Date of birth: 1 May 2002
Place of birth: The city of Tyumen, Russia
Family: He's the youngest son with lots of brothers and sisters
Top football skills: Speed and dribbling
Goal celebration: Sliding on his knees and howling
Likes to: Wear cool sports glasses when he's playing

© FIFA TM

Which winners?

Five of these nations have won the FIFA World Cup in the past. Place a FIFA World Cup Trophy sticker next to their names.

 Argentina

 Netherlands

 Italy

 Belgium

 Germany

 Spain

 France

The answers are at the back of the book.

ADD STICKER HERE

Sticker fun

There will be lots of places in your *Kids' Handbook* to place your cool FIFA World Cup stickers. Start by tackling the sticker quiz on this page.

Get to Know Russia

Russia is so excited to be staging the FIFA World Cup™ for the first time. The world's biggest country is ready to welcome the biggest football event and, even if its dream of winning the Trophy does not come true, it will be a competition full of skill, style, superstar players and spectacular action. Here is your quick guide to Russia!

Russia's record

Russia have appeared at ten FIFA World Cups, most recently in 2014 and 2002. Their best result was fourth place in 1966. In total Russia have played 40 FIFA World Cup tournament games, winning 17 and losing 15.

Great goalkeeper

Russia's greatest player was goalkeeper Lev Yashin, who went to four FIFA World Cups between 1958 and 1970. Yashin wore a black kit and got the nickname 'Black Spider' because he leaped around his area and liked to overpower strikers.

Double trouble

Russia have a pair of goalscorers that will give defenders nightmares. Artem Dzyuba is a giant striker who scored eight goals in qualifying for UEFA EURO 2016. He's added several more in friendlies, but was injured for the 2017 FIFA Confederations Cup. Fyodor Smolov did score at that tournament and now has nine goals in 26 games for Russia.

Fyodor Smolov was the Russian Premier League's top scorer in 2016-17.

Lev Yashin was an expert penalty saver who kept out around 150 penalties!

Go, go Golovin!

Aleksandr Golovin is one of Russia's brightest talents. The attacking midfielder scored in his first game for Russia in 2015, aged just 19. Golovin plays for CSKA Moscow and his skill, speed and quick thinking could make him a star at the 2018 FIFA World Cup.

Russian right or wrong?

	Right	Wrong
1. Aleksandr Kerzhakov scored a record 30 goals in 91 appearances for Russia between 2002 and 2016.		
2. Russia reached the semi-final of the 2006 and 2010 FIFA World Cups.		
3. The 2017 FIFA Confederations Cup was the first time Russia played in the tournament.		

The answers are at the back of the book.

Big and beautiful

At over 17 million square kilometres, Russia is the biggest country in the world – it's nearly twice the size of the USA! It has 143 million people and more than 100 languages are spoken. It has grand buildings like the Winter Palace, the Kremlin and St Basil's Cathedral. Russia is famous for producing amazing artists, such as writer Leo Tolstoy and ballet dancer Vaslav Nijinsky. The matryoshka doll, also called the Russian doll, is a well-known cultural symbol of Russia.

Country count

Russia is so vast that it shares borders with 14 different countries, including China, Poland, Ukraine, Mongolia, Georgia and Kazakhstan. It is in two continents, Europe and Asia, and the huge Mount Elbrus is the highest point in Europe.

Moscow's world-famous St Basil's Cathedral was built between 1555 and 1561.

Trophy Time

The FIFA World Cup Trophy is not the only award up for grabs in Russia. From top keepers to hotshot strikers, here is a look at some of the other prizes at the 2018 FIFA World Cup™.

FIFA World Cup Trophy

Very few players get to hold the golden FIFA World Cup Trophy. The original trophy was called the Jules Rimet Trophy and Brazil kept it after winning it for the third time in 1970. Sadly the Trophy was stolen in 1983 and never seen again. Today's Trophy is 36.8cm tall, weighs 6kg and is made of 18-carat gold.

2010 FIFA World Cup South Africa

adidas Golden Boot

Every striker dreams of winning this famous trophy, which is awarded to the top scorer in a FIFA World Cup. Germany's Thomas Müller took it in 2010, while Colombia forward James Rodríguez won it in 2014.

Teams that win the FIFA World Cup Trophy get to keep a gold-plated replica of it.

Hyundai Young Player Award

Players 21 years old or younger have a chance to be voted the top young star of a FIFA World Cup. France midfielder Paul Pogba lifted the award in 2014. Germany have had two recent winners with Thomas Müller in 2010 and Lukas Podolski in 2006.

Paul Pogba also won the adidas Golden Ball at the FIFA U-20 World Cup 2013.

adidas Golden Ball

This award is given to the player who has impressed the most at a FIFA World Cup. Lionel Messi won it in 2014 as he scored four goals and helped Argentina reach their first Final since 1990. Past winners include Germany goalkeeper Oliver Kahn, Brazil's Ronaldo and Romário, and France playmaker Zinedine Zidane.

James Rodríguez scored six goals to win the 2014 adidas Golden Boot.

adidas Golden Glove

This award goes to the best goalkeeper, who needs to have made lots of saves and helped his team to some big wins. Germany's Manuel Neuer scooped it in 2014 and Spain's Iker Casillas and Italy's Gianluigi Buffon have won it too.

Trophy talk

Draw a line linking the player to the trophy that he is talking about.

1. James Rodríguez, Colombia: "A dream come true."

2. Manuel Neuer, Germany: "We've wanted it for so long."

3. Paul Pogba, France: "I'm very proud to receive this award."

A

B

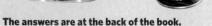

C

Manuel Neuer holds the 2014 adidas Golden Glove.

The answers are at the back of the book.

How the FIFA World Cup™ Works

Once the 31 qualifying teams were decided, they joined hosts Russia in knowing their spot at the 2018 FIFA World Cup was secure. The 32 nations will play at least three games each. The two teams that battle through the group and knockout stages will have to play six games to reach the Final. Then they could be just 90 minutes away from the ultimate prize – the FIFA World Cup Trophy!

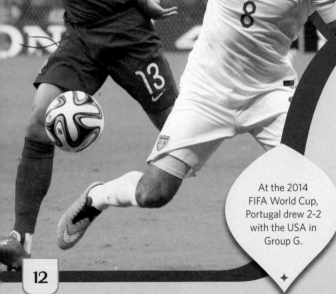

Group stages

The best eight teams are kept apart in the group stage, which has eight groups of four teams (see pages 42-43). Teams are drawn against others from around the world, although some groups will contain two teams from Europe. Teams play each other in their group and the top two will go through to the round of 16.

Round of 16

The top team in each group plays the runner-up from another, which makes eight matches. If a round of 16 game is tied at the end of 90 minutes, 30 minutes of extra time will be played. If the score is still level, a penalty shoot-out will decide the winner.

Quarter-finals

There are four quarter-finals, which again could go to extra time and a penalty shoot-out. They will be played in the cities of Sochi, Kazan, Nizhny Novgorod and Samara. Incredibly, only once have Germany failed to reach the last eight of a FIFA World Cup they have taken part in – and that was in 1938!

At the 2014 FIFA World Cup, Portugal drew 2-2 with the USA in Group G.

Semi-finals

The semi-finals are very dramatic because just one goal could send a country through to the Final. Probably the most famous FIFA World Cup semi-final took place in 2014 when Germany beat Brazil 7-1! Three of the last ten semi-finals have gone to extra time, so be prepared for tension and excitement.

Thomas Müller scores in Germany's famous 7-1 win over Brazil.

Moscow's Luzhniki Stadium will host the Final on 15 July.

© FIFA TM

Zabivaka says:
The losing teams in the semi-finals then play each other to see who finishes third.

The Final

The FIFA World Cup Final is the biggest single sporting event in the world – over 1 billion people watched some coverage of it in 2014! It is the same as all the other matches, with the final two teams left in the competition trying to win in 90 minutes. Only twice, in 1994 and 2006, has the Final been decided with a penalty shoot-out after extra time.

Paying the penalty

These players have all taken penalties in a FIFA World Cup Final shoot-out, but did they score? Use your tick stickers to decide.

1. David Trezeguet, France, 2006

(✓) Scored   (✓) Did not score

2. Dunga, Brazil, 1994

(✓) Scored   (✓) Did not score

3. Roberto Baggio, Italy, 1994

(✓) Scored   (✓) Did not score

The answers are at the back of the book.

© FIFA TM

Magical Moments

Ever since the first FIFA World Cup™ in 1930, there have been stacks of magical moments and special celebrations. From glorious goals to silky skills, great teams and individual players have lit up the 20 FIFA World Cup tournaments.

© FIFA TM

ZABIVAKA SAYS:
Brazil hero Ronaldo scored 15 FIFA World Cup tournament goals – five times more than Portugal's Cristiano Ronaldo has managed!

Brilliant Brazil

At the 1970 FIFA World Cup, Brazil scored probably the best goal ever seen in a Final. Captain Carlos Alberto crashed in a right-footed rocket shot from the edge of the penalty area to finish a flowing team move as Brazil beat Italy 4-1.

ADD STICKER HERE

Rocking Ronaldo

Striker Ronaldo (*left*) scored both of Brazil's goals against Germany to win the 2002 FIFA World Cup Final. It was consolation for the 1998 Final, when Ronaldo had a poor game as Brazil lost to France.

Awesome Owen

Aged just 18, England striker Michael Owen (*right*) ripped through Argentina's tough defence at the 1998 FIFA World Cup. He collected the ball in the centre circle, slid past two defenders in the blink of an eye, then fired the ball high into the net. England eventually lost on penalties but fans will never forget Owen's awesome strike.

ADD STICKER HERE

Cool Cruyff

Netherlands legend Johan Cruyff lit up the 1974 FIFA World Cup. After controlling the ball near Sweden's penalty area, Cruyff beat a defender by turning the ball behind his own standing foot, then sent in a cross. The defender looked dazed and the famous move was later called the 'Cruyff turn'.

Classy Cambiasso

Argentina have won the FIFA World Cup twice, in 1978 and 1986, and in 2006 they created something special too. Against Serbia & Montenegro, midfielder Esteban Cambiasso (*above*) scored a superb team goal after a clever 24-pass move that lasted 56 seconds.

True or false?

It's time for a quick test about three more fantastic FIFA World Cup moments.

1. In 1966, England's Geoff Hurst became the only player to score a hat-trick (three goals) in a FIFA World Cup Final.

True   False

2. In 1998, France's Laurent Blanc scored the first 'golden goal' at a FIFA World Cup. A 'golden goal' was a sudden-death goal scored in extra time that ended a match.

True   False

3. Hungary's László Kiss scored five goals after coming on as a substitute against El Salvador in 1982.

True   False

The answers are at the back of the book.

Close-up on the Coaches

The players on the pitch will make headlines with their goals, skills, passing and tackling, but the coach of each team is vitally important too. He picks the squad of 23 players, organizes the team for each game and chooses the tactics and substitutions. To win the Trophy, a top-quality coach is just as important as a star striker!

© FIFA TM

ZABIVAKA SAYS:
Only two people have won the FIFA World Cup as player and coach – Mário Zagallo (Brazil) and Franz Beckenbauer (Germany).

The lowdown on Löw

After winning the 2014 FIFA World Cup™, the 2017 FIFA Confederations Cup and finishing as runner-up at UEFA EURO 2008, Joachim Löw is already a legend in Germany. Löw has made the current world champions tough to beat with attacking talent throughout the team.

Martínez's moment?

Belgium's best FIFA World Cup performance was reaching the semi-finals in 1986. But coach Roberto Martínez has amazing stars such as Eden Hazard, Romelu Lukaku and Kevin de Bruyne, and could guide Belgium to their first Final appearance.

Terrific Tite

Adenor Bacchi, better known as Tite, became Brazil's head coach in 2016. He guided the team to nine qualifying wins in a row to become the first team, apart from Russia, to reach the 2018 FIFA World Cup. Tite has made Brazil strong in defence and has got the best out of players such as Marquinhos, Paulinho and Gabriel Jesus.

```
B E D M Z G S M I B I Q U
S I S C D M E X F Q T V I
Y E S O D I R J M X M Y D
M U P Q L M R Z X A D V C
Z Ü Q M U K O H R B O T L
M Z L Q E A T A N F Z D W
U K T L U K D S O L R A C
A B A K E O A X E A J M T
Q R K X N R S C J O F L H
E S J A Q I D R B Z K G K
V L V U Q M H V K P B I P
R A M S E Y E I E W G P M
Z P H X O R W W R N I P P
V K K F N Z I Y O K J I D
S U R F V Q R T O Y C L V
V F Y Q P N L C M R H L K
X H T C I T O G M H W M Z
I R A L O C S H Z I L F F
H H D T C K A N L O K S W
Q E L Z X L E I F V U K I
R D N C E U Q S O B L E D
U G D R T O Y F H X C I P
L O E O Y F P G V C D F O
I D K R E X Z Z F R U L E
U W G Z F I T T O T L N N
```

FIFA World Cup™ word search

These coaches and players have all won the FIFA World Cup, but can you find their surnames hiding in the grid?

Coaches

Alf **Ramsey**

Vicente **del Bosque**

Marcello **Lippi**

Luiz Felipe **Scolari**

Players

Gerd **Müller**

Mario **Kempes**

Philipp **Lahm**

Bobby **Moore**

Miroslav **Klose**

Diego **Maradona**

Fernando **Torres**

Roberto **Carlos**

Thierry **Henry**

Francesco **Totti**

The answers are at the back of the book.

17

Stadium Spotlight

There are 12 amazing stadiums being used for the 2018 FIFA World Cup™. Eight awesome new stadiums have been built, two have been adapted from other sporting events, and the final two are existing stadiums in Moscow.

Ekaterinburg Arena

City: Ekaterinburg
Capacity: 35,696
FIFA World Cup matches: Four group games.
Did you know? This stadium was completed in 1957 and last updated in 2011. A roof and temporary stand will be installed for Russia 2018.

Kaliningrad Stadium

City: Kaliningrad
Capacity: 35,212
FIFA World Cup matches: Four group games.
Did you know? This new stadium has been built on Oktyabrsky Island. After Russia 2018 it will host FC Baltika Kaliningrad games.

Mordovia Arena

City: Saransk
Capacity: 44,442
FIFA World Cup matches: Four group games.
Did you know? Probably Russia's brightest stadium, its mix of orange, red and white reflects the arts and crafts of this part of western Russia.

Luzhniki Stadium

City: Moscow
Capacity: 81,000
FIFA World Cup matches: Seven, including Russia's opening match and the Final.
Did you know? This famous old stadium has hosted the Olympics and a UEFA Champions League final.

Spartak Stadium

City: Moscow
Capacity: 43,298
FIFA World Cup matches: Four group games and one round of 16 match.
Did you know? Its outer skin is made from diamond shapes that change colour to match the teams that are playing.

Kazan Arena

City: Kazan
Capacity: 44,779
FIFA World Cup matches: Six, including one quarter-final.
Did you know? The Kazan Arena might look familiar because it was designed by the same people who built Wembley Stadium.

The Saint Petersburg Stadium hosted the final of the 2017 FIFA Confederations Cup.

Fisht Stadium

City: Sochi

Capacity: 47,659

FIFA World Cup matches: Six, including one quarter-final.

Did you know? The Fisht Stadium was built for the 2014 Winter Olympics. Its shape is modelled on a snowy white mountain!

Samara Arena

City: Samara

Capacity: 44,807

FIFA World Cup matches: Six, including four group games.

Did you know? Its design is based on the region's links to space travel, with giant glass panels that light up and look like a spacecraft.

Rostov Arena

City: Rostov-on-Don

Capacity: 45,145

FIFA World Cup matches: Four group games and one round of 16 match.

Did you know? Its ultra-modern roof design reflects the twists and turns of the Don River next to the stadium.

Saint Petersburg Stadium

City: Saint Petersburg

Capacity: 68,134

FIFA World Cup matches: Seven, including one semi-final.

Did you know? It has a sliding roof and pitch, and even in winter the temperature can be controlled at 15°C.

Volgograd Arena

City: Volgograd

Capacity: 45,568

FIFA World Cup matches: Four group games.

Did you know? It was designed to look both mechanical, like the spokes on a bicycle wheel, and artistic with its upside-down cone shape.

Nizhny Novgorod Stadium

City: Nizhny Novgorod

Capacity: 45,331

FIFA World Cup matches: Six, including one quarter-final.

Did you know? It has beautiful views of the Volga and Oka rivers and the Alexander Nevsky Cathedral.

Code Cracker Quiz

Zabivaka has created football codes so you can crack these awesome FIFA World Cup™ quizzes. Follow Zabivaka's rules and write down your answers.

Letter game

This FIFA World Cup star's name is written in code. Under each letter, write the letter that actually goes before it in the alphabet to reveal the real player.

O F Z N B S

Close call

This goal ace can only be seen in close-up images. Study the photos and choose who you think it is from the options below.

Is it...

Harry Kane

Antoine Griezmann

Isco

Mesut Özil

Figure it out

To disguise this famous FIFA World Cup country, its name has been written in numbers. Follow these rules and guess which country it could be.

1 = One of the letters from A to E;
2 = F to K; **3 =** L to Q; **4 =** R to V

4 3 1 2 3

Super strikers

Time to work out which goalscorers are being described here, just from the list of clubs they have played for. If you need help, look at the players to choose from at the bottom.

CLUBS:
Sporting Lisbon
Manchester United
Real Madrid
The player is:

....

CLUBS:
Nacional
Groningen
Ajax
Liverpool
Barcelona
The player is:

....

CLUBS:
River Plate
Real Madrid
Napoli
Juventus
The player is:

....

CLUBS:
Mainz 05
Bayer Leverkusen
Chelsea
Wolfsburg
Borussia Dortmund
The player is:

....

Choose from: André Schürrle
Gonzalo Higuaín
Luis Suárez
Cristiano Ronaldo

Number crunch

Find the right stickers to fill in the missing number from the year of each tournament.

1. **197** (?)
   In this year the FIFA World Cup was held in Argentina.

2. **200** (?)
   One of the mascots this year was a lion called Goleo.

3. **199** (?)
   In this year, all four teams in Group E won four points.

The answers are at the back of the book.

21

Champions!

The FIFA World Cup™ holders are Germany, who beat Argentina 1-0 in 2014. Just seven other nations have been crowned world champions. Here are the eight countries lucky enough to get their hands on the golden Trophy since 1930...

Italy's Fabio Cannavaro lifts the Trophy in 2006.

Germany

Winners: 2014, 1990, 1974, 1954

Germany boast the best record of all European teams at the FIFA World Cup. They have featured in 18 tournaments, played in a record eight Finals and been victorious four times.

Argentina

Winners: 1986, 1978

Argentina lost in the first FIFA World Cup Final, in 1930, and had to wait 48 years to finally lift the Trophy. They repeated their win just eight years later in Mexico.

England

Winners: 1966

The host nation has won the FIFA World Cup six times. England did just that at Wembley Stadium in 1966, dramatically beating West Germany 4-2 in extra time.

Italy

Winners: 2006, 1982, 1938, 1934

Along with Brazil, Italy are the only country to win two FIFA World Cup Finals in a row. The Italians have triumphed four times and twice finished second, in 1970 and 1994.

Brazil

Winners: 2002, 1994, 1970, 1962, 1958

Brazil are the only country with five FIFA World Cup titles. They have been runners-up twice, and have picked up a record 227 points at the Finals. Brazil have also played in every tournament.

Uruguay

Winners: 1950, 1930

The South Americans won the Jules Rimet Trophy in their own country in 1930 and then stunned Brazil, in Rio, 20 years later to do it again.

France

Winners: 1998

At the Stade de France, the hosts demolished Brazil 3-0 in the 1998 Final thanks to two goals from Zinedine Zidane and Emmanuel Petit's injury-time strike. The party in Paris went on for hours after the final whistle!

Spain

Winners: 2010

Andrés Iniesta was Spain's hero at South Africa 2010. His late extra-time goal secured the country's first ever win in the Final as Vicente del Bosque's team won their last four matches 1-0.

Spot the difference

Can you find six differences between these two pictures of Germany celebrating their 2014 FIFA World Cup victory?

The answers are at the back of the book.

2014 FIFA World Cup™ Champions

REUS 21

CHAMPIONS
2014 FIFA World Cup™

2010 FIFA World Cup™ Champions

REUS 22

CHAMPIONS
2014 FIFA World Cup™

Fab Formations

You have met some of the FIFA World Cup™ coaches, so now we can look at the tactics and formations they will use at the tournament. A coach can arrange his players in a variety of ways on the pitch, but these formations are the most popular.

England full-back Kyle Walker.

4-4-2

This is a classic and popular way to line up a team's 11 players. It uses four defenders (two centre-backs and two full-backs), four midfielders (two central and two wingers) and two strikers. It is a system that England have used many times and offers defensive security as well as attacking support. Obviously all these formations use one goalkeeper too!

4-2-3-1

With four defenders, two defensive midfielders, three forwards and a central striker, this formation is designed to keep a team strong at the back and powerful in attack. Spain and Brazil have used it to great effect at FIFA World Cups. The striker must be powerful, alert and able to link with the supporting midfielders and forwards.

Belgian wing-back Yannick Carrasco.

3-5-2

Wing-backs are the key to this formation. On the right and left, a wing-back must be able to burst forward, cross the ball and help set up attacks, but also get back to defend with the three centre-backs. If a team needs to score a goal towards the end of a game, it may use 3-5-2 to get players up the pitch near the opposition's goal.

© FIFA TM

Zabivaka says:

A team needing to protect a lead or play very defensively could use 4-5-1, with only one striker.

Tactical terms explained...

Playmaker:
A clever midfielder who passes well, sets up goals and controls the speed of the game.

False nine:
A striker that also drops into midfield to collect the ball and lose a defender marking him.

Sweeper keeper:
A goalkeeper that will come out of his area to kick the ball away and set his team on the attack.

Tactics test

These formations show 4-4-2 and 3-5-2. Read each clue, then write which formation goes with each.

A

Right and left wing-backs are used with this formation.

B

This formation uses two centre-backs and a right and left winger.

The answers are at the back of the book.

Player Watch: FORWARDS

There is a reason why goalscorers and strikers are the most expensive players to buy – they win games! It takes a special talent to put the ball in the net, especially under pressure in a big FIFA World Cup™ match. These five fearsome forwards will hope to score stacks of goals this summer.

© FIFA TM

Lionel Messi

Country: Argentina
Club: Barcelona
Born: 24 June 1987
Games: 122
Goals: 61

He's good at... Being the best in the world! Argentina captain Messi took his country to the 2014 FIFA World Cup Final and in 2018 he wants to finally win the Trophy. His left foot is lethal and from inside or outside the penalty area, Messi is a constant danger.

Harry Kane

Country: England
Club: Tottenham
Born: 28 July 1993
Games: 23
Goals: 12

He's good at... Scoring goals from anywhere! Kane is England's leading striker and has all the skills to become a FIFA World Cup star. He has power, speed, good footwork and loves to shoot from distance and surprise the goalkeeper. The 2018 tournament is Kane's first FIFA World Cup.

Harry Kane was the Premier League's top scorer in both 2015-16 and 2016-17.

Neymar

Country: Brazil
Club: Paris Saint-Germain
Born: 5 February 1992
Games: 81
Goals: 52

He's good at... Driving and dribbling into the penalty area. Neymar helped Brazil reach the semi-finals in 2014 and after joining PSG from Barcelona for a record €222 million, all eyes will be on him. The forward has a deadly mix of shooting, free kick and crossing skills.

Surprisingly Cristiano Ronaldo only has three goals from 13 FIFA World Cup Finals matches.

Romelu Lukaku

Country: Belgium
Club: Manchester United
Born: 13 May 1993
Games: 63
Goals: 28

He's good at... Powering past defenders. Lukaku's big move to Manchester United in 2017 gave him the stage to display his predatory goal skills. He scored 11 goals in eight games to help Belgium reach Russia 2018, and he will be a big threat for defenders with his speed and laser-guided shooting.

Cristiano Ronaldo

Country: Portugal
Club: Real Madrid
Born: 5 February 1985
Games: 145
Goals: 79

He's good at... Everything! Ronaldo has the strength and speed to play as a central striker, and the silky skills to dazzle out wide and cross or dribble into the box. Portugal have never reached the Final but with Ronaldo in attack they have every chance at Russia 2018.

Player Watch:
MIDFIELDERS

Shooting, tackling, passing, running, crossing – these are all skills that a top midfield master needs to compete at the FIFA World Cup™ Finals! Luckily the five midfielders here have all these powers, and loads more, so the *Kids' Handbook* reveals the guys to keep an eye on in Russia.

Eden's younger brother, Thorgan, also plays for the Belgian national team.

Eden Hazard

Country: Belgium
Club: Chelsea
Born: 7 January 1991
Games: 81
Goals: 20

He's good at... Frightening the life out of defenders! Hazard is the complete attacking midfielder – he can pass, shoot, dribble, take free kicks, score from distance and tuck away penalties. He's one of the most exciting players in the world.

Philippe Coutinho

Country: Brazil
Club: Liverpool
Born: 12 June 1992
Games: 31
Goals: 8

He's good at... Playing perfect passes from his attacking midfield position, setting up goals and dribbling past defenders. Coutinho's long-range shooting and fierce free kicks are awesomely accurate too!

Coutinho's first Brazil hat-trick came in a 7-1 *Copa América* win over Haiti in 2016.

Mesut Özil

Country: Germany
Club: Arsenal
Born: 15 October 1988
Games: 86
Goals: 22

He's good at... Setting up goals! When Germany won the 2014 FIFA World Cup, Özil made two assists and he also has an epic 42 assists in 121 Premier League games for Arsenal. He's a goal creating, and goalscoring, machine!

Paul Pogba

Country: France
Club: Manchester United
Born: 15 March 1993
Games: 49
Goals: 8

He's good at... Powering forwards and scoring goals. Pogba has incredible strength and loves to win a tackle, drive into the box and set up attacks. He's comfortable with both feet and is a strong header of the ball.

Pogba was the first player in the world to be sold for more than €100 million.

Dele Alli

Country: England
Club: Tottenham
Born: 11 April 1996
Games: 22
Goals: 2

He's good at... Supporting the strikers. Alli has quick feet and a sharp brain, which means he will create goals for the forwards and loves to shoot at the keeper too.

Alli's full name is Bamidele Jermaine Alli. He turned professional aged just 16.

Player Watch:
DEFENDERS

Having reliable, experienced and alert defenders helps a country go a long way at the FIFA World Cup™. These five fearsome defenders love completing 90 minutes without letting in a goal. They are a danger from corners and free kicks, too, as their height and power threatens the opposition's goal.

Ramos won nine of his 13 FIFA World Cup Finals games between 2006 and 2014.

Sergio Ramos

Country: Spain
Club: Real Madrid
Born: 30 March 1986
Games: 147
Goals: 11

He's good at... Stopping, and scoring, goals! Ramos is one of the world's most formidable centre-backs with speed, style and a strong will to win. He enjoys battling strikers and has a knack of scoring important goals too. He was a FIFA World Cup winner with Spain in 2010.

Diego Godín

Country: Uruguay
Club: Atlético Madrid
Born: 16 February 1986
Games: 113
Goals: 8

He's good at... Organizing his defence. The tall centre-back is a powerful header of the ball and a master at stealing the ball from strikers. Godín has won the UEFA Europa League and *La Liga* with Atlético Madrid, and now he wants glory at Russia 2018!

Jan Vertonghen

Country: Belgium
Club: Tottenham
Born: 24 April 1987
Games: 97
Goals: 8

He's good at... Overpowering strikers. Vertonghen knows exactly when, and how, to steal the ball from the opposition and shut down danger. Playing alongside his Tottenham team-mate Toby Alderweireld, he helped Belgium concede just six goals in qualifying.

Dani Alves

Country: Brazil
Club: Paris Saint-Germain
Born: 6 May 1983
Games: 105
Goals: 7

He's good at... Winning! Alves has won La Liga, UEFA Champions League, *Copa América* and the FIFA Confederations Cup, but Russia 2018 is his last chance to lift the FIFA World Cup Trophy. The right-back is a tough tackler and is superb from dead-ball situations.

Raphaël Varane

Country: France
Club: Real Madrid
Born: 25 April 1993
Games: 39 **Goals:** 2

He's good at... Whisking the ball away from opponents. Varane played all five games for France at Brazil 2014 and his leadership and power will be important if *Les Bleus* are to reach the knockout stage in Russia.

Varane has never received a yellow card in 15 FIFA World Cup Finals and qualifying games.

© FIFA TM

ZABIVAKA SAYS:
In 2006, Italy's Fabio Cannavaro became the first defender to win FIFA's Ballon d'Or best player award.

Player Watch:
GOALKEEPERS

© FIFA TM

Having a 'safe pair of hands' between the goalposts is what all FIFA World Cup™ coaches dream of. Luckily, these goalkeepers are some of the very best! From shot-stopping to punching and catching the ball, plus kicking it huge distances down the pitch, these keepers have what it takes for success at Russia 2018.

Manuel Neuer

Country: Germany
Club: Bayern Munich
Born: 27 March 1986
Games: 74
Goals: 0

He's good at... Commanding his area. With his powerful kicking and strong handling, Neuer is the undisputed German Number 1. His defenders know he can race from his line and clear danger, then quickly set up an attack. Germany's captain fancies his chances of winning back-to-back FIFA World Cups!

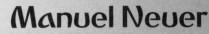

Hugo Lloris

Country: France
Club: Tottenham
Born: 26 December 1986
Games: 94
Goals: 0

He's good at... Blocking strikers in one-on-one situations. Lloris has nearly 100 caps for France and uses all his experience to marshal the backline – he is not afraid to give defenders a loud talking to! He has never gone past the quarter-finals though, and this time the captain has the Final in his sight.

Keylor Navas

Country: Costa Rica
Club: Real Madrid
Born: 15 December 1986
Games: 76
Goals: 0

He's good at... Keeping clean sheets at the FIFA World Cup! At Brazil 2014, Navas was a star for Costa Rica as they reached the quarter-finals. The Real Madrid ace kept three clean sheets in five games with his athletic saves and ice-cool concentration.

David de Gea

Country: Spain
Club: Manchester United
Born: 7 November 1990
Games: 24
Goals: 0

He's good at... Flying through the air to block shots. Spain are lucky to have De Gea in goal because his agility and superhuman saves help them win lots of games. In De Gea's nine Russia 2018 qualifiers he conceded just three goals.

The 2018 FIFA World Cup Finals will be De Gea's first ever.

Łukasz Fabiański

Country: Poland
Club: Swansea City
Born: 18 April 1985
Games: 41
Goals: 0

He's good at... Surprising opponents with stunning saves! Fabiański is a great all-round goalkeeper with robot-like reflexes and a strong presence. He will battle Wojciech Szczesny to be Poland's Number 1 at Russia 2018.

Easy as... A, B, C

Here is Hugo Lloris in action for France. Which ball is the correct one, though? Put a tick sticker next to A, B or C.

 A B C

The answers are at the back of the book.

33

Year We Go

Your knowledge of the FIFA World Cup™ should be pretty sharp by now! To see how much you know, here is a quick tournament test. All you have to do is write the correct year next to the question. If you need some help, take a look at the list of all 20 FIFA World Cup Finals from 1930 to 2014.

South Korea celebrate a shock 2-1 victory over Italy on their way to the semi-finals.

1. Striker Davor Šuker was the surprise winner of the adidas Golden Boot top scorer award this year. His Croatia team finished third, behind France and Brazil.

Year:

2. In this year, Germany and Brazil both played their 100th FIFA World Cup Finals match.

Year:

3. Netherlands played the first of their three FIFA World Cup Finals, all of which they lost, in this year.

Year:

4. This FIFA World Cup Final had the highest attendance, with over 200,000 fans watching hosts Brazil play Uruguay. Can you name the year?

Year:

Croatia's Davor Šuker scored six goals to win the adidas Golden Boot.

© FIFA TM

ZABIVAKA SAYS:
Nine players have scored FIFA World Cup Finals goals 12 years apart, including Miroslav Klose, Pelé, Michael Laudrup, Maradona and Henrik Larsson.

5. France's Lucien Laurent is famous for being the first ever scorer of a FIFA World Cup goal. In which year was that?

Year:

....

6. In this year, the FIFA World Cup Final was the first not to feature Brazil, Italy, Germany or Argentina.

Year:

....

7. Turkey and co-hosts South Korea were shock semi-finalists at this FIFA World Cup.

Year:

....

8. This was a famous year for Italian coach Vittorio Pozzo. He guided his country to its second FIFA World Cup Final win in a row.

Year:

....

The answers are at the back of the book.

Every FIFA World Cup™ Final...

1930	Uruguay 4-2 Argentina
1934	Italy 2-1 Czechoslovakia
1938	Italy 4-2 Hungary
1950	Uruguay 2-1 Brazil
1954	West Germany 3-2 Hungary
1958	Brazil 5-2 Sweden
1962	Brazil 3-1 Czechoslovakia
1966	England 4-2 West Germany
1970	Brazil 4-1 Italy
1974	West Germany 2-1 Netherlands
1978	Argentina 3-1 Netherlands
1982	Italy 3-1 West Germany
1986	Argentina 3-2 West Germany
1990	West Germany 1-0 Argentina
1994	Brazil 0-0 Italy*
1998	France 3-0 Brazil
2002	Brazil 2-0 Germany
2006	Italy 1-1 France**
2010	Spain 1-0 Netherlands
2014	Germany 1-0 Argentina

* Brazil won 3-2 on penalties
** Italy won 5-3 on penalties

Sweden's Henrik Larsson scored at the 1994, 2002 and 2006 FIFA World Cups.

FIFA World Cup™ Heroes

A country needs reliable strikers, tough defenders, classy midfielders and a great goalkeeper to win the FIFA World Cup. These five FIFA World Cup winners all have amazing records at the Finals.

ZABIVAKA SAYS:
England's top FIFA World Cup Finals scorer is Gary Lineker, with ten goals. His six strikes in 1986 won the adidas Golden Boot.

Miroslav Klose

Country: Germany
FIFA World Cup Finals games/goals: 24/16

At the 2014 FIFA World Cup, Miroslav Klose scored a record 16th tournament goal. That was also the year that he won the Trophy for the first time, having been a runner-up in 2002. Klose also won the adidas Golden Boot thanks to his five strikes at the 2006 tournament, and is Germany's top goalscorer with an amazing 71 goals.

Klose scored his first FIFA World Cup Finals goal in 2002 and his last in 2014.

Maradona won the adidas Golden Ball award as best player in the 1986 Finals.

Diego Maradona

Country: Argentina
FIFA World Cup Finals games/goals: 21/8

The legendary Argentina ace captained his country to glory in the 1986 FIFA World Cup and also played in the 1982, 1990 and 1994 tournaments. He scored two goals against England in the quarter-final in 1986 – one was a handball, known as the Hand of God, but the second was a superb solo run and finish in the penalty box.

Dino Zoff

Country: Italy
FIFA World Cup Finals games/goals: 17/0

Aged 40 years, four months and 11 days, goalkeeper Dino Zoff is the oldest player to captain a FIFA World Cup-winning team. That honour came in 1982, and Zoff also played in the 1970, 1974 and 1978 tournaments. His commanding style between the posts meant Zoff lost only three of the 17 Finals games he played in.

Pelé

Country: Brazil
FIFA World Cup Finals games/goals: 14/12

Crowned FIFA Player of the Century in 2000 alongside Maradona, Pelé is a hero in Brazil. He won the FIFA World Cup in 1958, 1962 and 1970, and scored an incredible 12 goals in just 14 Finals games. Pelé's first victory in a Final came when he was just 17.

Zinedine Zidane

Country: France
FIFA World Cup Finals games/goals: 12/5

With two goals in the 1998 FIFA World Cup Final, Zinedine Zidane will always be remembered as a legend at the tournament. The attacking midfielder had magical skills and vision, and came out of retirement to lead France to another Final in 2006, when they lost to Italy on penalties.

Zidane is the oldest player to win the adidas Golden Ball, at the age of 34.

Find the flag

Place each of your three flag stickers by the correct FIFA World Cup legend.

1. Just Fontaine scored 13 goals in just six FIFA World Cup Finals games for this country.

2. Lothar Matthäus played in 25 FIFA World Cup Finals matches, but for which country?

3. Romário won the FIFA World Cup and adidas Golden Ball award playing for this nation.

The answers are at the back of the book.

Spot the Lot

If you are not able to attend games at Russia 2018, the next best thing is watching all the action and drama on TV and tablets. Use your tick stickers to mark each of these moments when you spot them at the FIFA World Cup™ Finals!

Russia will be full of colour and costumes as the fans celebrate.

ZABIVAKA SAYS:
Ten red cards were shown at the 2014 FIFA World Cup.

Fantastic fans

Lots of supporters at the FIFA World Cup dress up in colourful clothes, crazy glasses and wacky hats as they party at the stadiums. Keep your eyes peeled for these fantastic fans!

I SPOTTED IT!

Sad supporters

But sometimes when their team is losing, watching a game can be a bit upsetting too! Some supporters may shed a tear or two if their FIFA World Cup dream comes to an end.

 I SPOTTED IT!

Dancing stars

Footballers love to dance and celebrate after scoring a goal or winning a big game. The Samba boys of Brazil are famous for it!

 I SPOTTED IT!

Captain calling

Whether a team is winning or losing, it is the captain's job to give instructions to the other players on the pitch and to make sure everyone is trying hard. Can you spot a captain getting in the ear of his team-mates?

 I SPOTTED IT!

Trophy parade

On 15 July, the 2018 FIFA World Cup winners will proudly display the Trophy as they celebrate on the Luzhniki Stadium pitch. As soon as you spot it, place your sticker here!

 I SPOTTED IT!

Zabivaka out and about

Zabivaka, the Russia 2018 mascot, will appear on the pitch at all the group and knockout stage matches. Make sure you see the football-crazy wolf!

 I SPOTTED IT!

Red alert

It is very likely that a referee will show a red card at the Finals, which means a player will have been sent off. Watch out for red in Russia!

 I SPOTTED IT!

Penalty pressure

One of the most exciting moments at a FIFA World Cup can be a penalty shoot-out. If you see players lining up to take a pressure-packed penalty in a knockout game, mark it here.

 I SPOTTED IT!

Argentina's Sergio Agüero scores in a shoot-out win over the Netherlands in 2014.

© FIFA TM

FIFA World Cup™ Record Breakers

If you like numbers, stats and facts, you will love these FIFA World Cup record breakers! All of these players and teams have hit the headlines on the biggest football stage, from record goalscorers to golden oldies. Check them out and watch for more records being smashed at Russia 2018.

ZABIVAKA SAYS:
England and Italy have both lost a record three penalty shoot-outs at FIFA World Cups.

Goals galore

A record 171 goals were scored at both the 2014 and 1998 FIFA World Cups. There were just 70 strikes in 1930 and 1934.

Robin van Persie's diving header against Spain was voted the third-best goal in 2014.

Great Germany

Germany have scored a record 224 goals at FIFA World Cup tournaments, which is more than Brazil, Italy and Argentina. Gerd Müller hit 14 in only 13 games at the 1970 and 1974 tournaments.

Mega minutes

Former Italy captain Paolo Maldini holds the record for playing the most minutes at FIFA World Cup Finals. The defender played for 2,217 minutes across four tournaments between 1990 and 2002.

Hat-trick hero

Hungary goal machine László Kiss scored a hat-trick (three goals) in a record-breaking eight minutes against El Salvador at the 1982 tournament. Kiss also became the only substitute to hit three goals at the Finals.

Golden oldie

The oldest player at a FIFA World Cup was Faryd Mondragon. The Colombia goalkeeper was 43 years and three days old when he played at Brazil 2014.

Super Salenko

Oleg Salenko is the only player to score five goals in a FIFA World Cup Finals match – against Cameroon at USA 1994. Despite this amazing feat, he never played for Russia again.

Terrific 12

The highest-scoring game at a FIFA World Cup was in 1954 when Austria beat Switzerland 7-5.

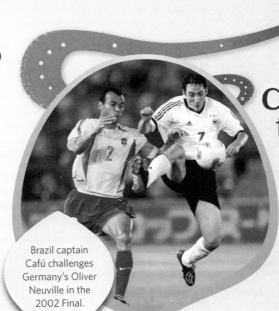

Brazil captain Cafú challenges Germany's Oliver Neuville in the 2002 Final.

Captain fantastic

Legendary Brazil right-back Cafú is the only player to appear in three FIFA World Cup Finals: 1994, 1998 and 2002. He captained Brazil to the Trophy in the last.

Spot the ball

Mexico striker Javier Hernández scored one of the record-equalling 171 goals at Brazil 2014. Here he is scoring against Croatia, but which is the original ball?

The answers are at the back of the book.

The Group Stage

Fill in the results from the matches as they are played and record the progress of all 32 teams. Who will lift the FIFA World Cup Trophy at the Luzhniki Stadium on 15 July?

Group A

14 June, 18:00	Russia			....	Moscow (Luzhniki)
15 June, 17:00	....			....	Ekaterinburg
19 June, 21:00	Russia			....	Saint Petersburg
20 June, 18:00	....			....	Rostov-on-Don
25 June, 18:00				Russia	Samara
25 June, 17:00	....			....	Volgograd

Team	P	W	D	L	GD	Pts

Group B

15 June, 21:00	....			....	Sochi
15 June, 18:00	....			....	Saint Petersburg
20 June, 15:00	....			....	Moscow (Luzhniki)
20 June, 21:00	....			....	Kazan
25 June, 21:00	....			....	Saransk
25 June, 20:00	....			....	Kaliningrad

Team	P	W	D	L	GD	Pts

Group C

16 June, 13:00	....			....	Kazan
16 June, 19:00	....			....	Saransk
21 June, 17:00	....			....	Ekaterinburg
21 June, 19:00	....			....	Samara
26 June, 17:00	....			....	Moscow (Luzhniki)
26 June, 17:00	....			....	Sochi

Team	P	W	D	L	GD	Pts

Group D

16 June, 16:00	....			....	Moscow (Spartak)
16 June, 21:00	....			....	Kaliningrad
21 June, 21:00	....			....	Nizhny Novgorod
22 June, 18:00	....			....	Volgograd
26 June, 21:00	....			....	Saint Petersburg
26 June, 21:00	....			....	Rostov-on-Don

Team	P	W	D	L	GD	Pts

NOTE: ALL TIMES ARE LOCAL TIMES.

© FIFA TM

Group E

17 June, 16:00	.... ☐ ☐	Samara
17 June, 21:00	.... ☐ ☐	Rostov-on-Don
22 June, 15:00	.... ☐ ☐	Saint Petersburg
22 June, 20:00	.... ☐ ☐	Kaliningrad
27 June, 21:00	.... ☐ ☐	Moscow (Spartak)
27 June, 21:00	.... ☐ ☐	Nizhny Novgorod

— ◆ —

Team	P	W	D	L	GD	Pts

Group F

17 June, 18:00	.... ☐ ☐	Moscow (Luzhniki)
18 June, 15:00	.... ☐ ☐	Nizhny Novgorod
23 June, 18:00	.... ☐ ☐	Sochi
23 June, 21:00	.... ☐ ☐	Rostov-on-Don
27 June, 17:00	.... ☐ ☐	Kazan
27 June, 19:00	.... ☐ ☐	Ekaterinburg

— ◆ —

Team	P	W	D	L	GD	Pts

Group G

18 June, 18:00	.... ☐ ☐	Sochi
18 June, 21:00	.... ☐ ☐	Volgograd
23 June, 15:00	.... ☐ ☐	Moscow (Spartak)
24 June, 15:00	.... ☐ ☐	Nizhny Novgorod
28 June, 20:00	.... ☐ ☐	Kaliningrad
28 June, 21:00	.... ☐ ☐	Saransk

— ◆ —

Team	P	W	D	L	GD	Pts

Group H

19 June, 15:00	.... ☐ ☐	Moscow (Spartak)
19 June, 18:00	.... ☐ ☐	Saransk
24 June, 21:00	.... ☐ ☐	Kazan
24 June, 20:00	.... ☐ ☐	Ekaterinburg
28 June, 17:00	.... ☐ ☐	Volgograd
28 June, 18:00	.... ☐ ☐	Samara

— ◆ —

Team	P	W	D	L	GD	Pts

Round of 16

30 June, 21:00 — Match 49 — Sochi

Winner Group A — — Runner-up Group B

Goals:

Goals:

Cards:

Cards:

Man of the match:

30 June, 17:00 — Match 50 — Kazan

Winner Group C — — Runner-up Group D

Goals:

Goals:

Cards:

Cards:

Man of the match:

1 July, 17:00 — Match 51 — Moscow (Luzhniki)

Winner Group B — — Runner-up Group A

Goals:

Goals:

Cards:

Cards:

Man of the match:

1 July, 21:00 — Match 52 — Nizhny Novgorod

Winner Group D — — Runner-up Group C

Goals:

Goals:

Cards:

Cards:

Man of the match:

2 July, 18:00 — Match 53 — Samara

Winner Group E — — Runner-up Group F

Goals:

Goals:

Cards:

Cards:

Man of the match:

2 July, 21:00 — Match 54 — Rostov-on-Don

Winner Group G — — Runner-up Group H

Goals:

Goals:

Cards:

Cards:

Man of the match:

3 July, 17:00 — Match 55 — Saint Petersburg

Winner Group F — — Runner-up Group E

Goals:

Goals:

Cards:

Cards:

Man of the match:

3 July, 21:00 — Match 56 — Moscow (Spartak)

Winner Group H — — Runner-up Group G

Goals:

Goals:

Cards:

Cards:

Man of the match:

Quarter-Finals

6 July, 17:00 — Match 57 — Nizhny Novgorod

Winner match 49 — Winner match 50

Goals:

Goals:

Cards:

Cards:

Man of the match:

6 July, 21:00 — Match 58 — Kazan

Winner match 53 — Winner match 54

Goals:

Goals:

Cards:

Cards:

Man of the match:

7 July, 21:00 — Match 59 — Sochi

Winner match 51 — Winner match 52

Goals:

Goals:

Cards:

Cards:

Man of the match:

7 July, 18:00 — Match 60 — Samara

Winner match 55 — Winner match 56

Goals:

Goals:

Cards:

Cards:

Man of the match:

NOTE: ALL TIMES ARE LOCAL TIMES.

Semi-Finals

10 July, 21:00   Match 61   **Saint Petersburg**

Winner match 57   Winner match 58

—

Goals: Goals:

Cards: Cards:

Man of the match:

11 July, 21:00   Match 62   **Moscow (Luzhniki)**

Winner match 59   Winner match 60

—

Goals: Goals:

Cards: Cards:

Man of the match:

© FIFA TM

ZABIVAKA SAYS:

Germany hold the record for the most third-place finishes, with four in total.

Third-Place Play-off

14 July, 17:00   Match 63   **Saint Petersburg**

Runner-up match 61   Runner-up match 62

—

Goals: Goals:

Cards: Cards:

Man of the match:

NOTE: ALL TIMES ARE LOCAL TIMES.

FIFA World Cup™ Final

15 July, 18:00   Moscow (Luzhniki)

Score
–

Winner match 61

Line-up:

Substitutes:

Goals:

Cards:

Winner match 62

Line-up:

Substitutes:

Goals:

Cards:

Man of the Match:

Answers

Page 7: Which winners?
Argentina, Italy, Germany, Spain and France have all won the FIFA World Cup™.

Page 9: Russian right or wrong?
1. Right; 2. Wrong; 3. Right

Page 11: Trophy talk
1.C (adidas Golden Boot); 2.B (FIFA World Cup Trophy); 3.A (Hyundai Young Player Award)

Page 13: Paying the penalty
1. Did not score; 2. Scored; 3. Did not score

Page 15: True or false?
1. True; 2. True; 3. False (he scored three goals)

Page 20: Letter game
Neymar

Page 20: Close call
Antoine Griezmann

Page 20: Figure it out
Spain

Page 21: Super strikers
Cristiano Ronaldo; Luis Suárez; Gonzalo Higuaín; André Schürrle

Page 21: Number crunch
1. 1978; 2. 2006; 3. 1994

Page 25: Tactics test
A. 3-5-2; B. 4-4-2

Page 17: FIFA World Cup™ word search

Page 23: Spot the difference

Page 33: Easy as... A, B, C   Ball B

Page 41: Spot the ball

Page 34-35: Year we go
1. 1998; 2. 2014; 3. 1974; 4. 1950; 5. 1930; 6. 2010; 7. 2002; 8. 1938

Page 37: Find the flag
1. France; 2. Germany; 3. Brazil